2024 HONG KONG
TRAVEL GUIDE

Full-Color Pocket Travel Guide for First Timers Featuring Colored Pictures and City Maps

Richard Stephen

TABLE OF CONTENTS

1

INTRODUCTION

Stepping foot onto the lively streets of Hong Kong is like entering a pulsating symphony of commerce, culture and history. My journey to this dynamic city was a sensory overload—a whirlwind of sights, sounds, and flavors that captured my imagination from the moment I arrived.

From the iconic skyline defined by towering skyscrapers to the narrow alleyways brimming with local markets and the aromatic haze of steaming street food, every corner of Hong Kong tells a unique story. The blend of tradition and modernity here is seamless, where ancient temples stand in the shadows of contemporary architectural marvels, and time-honored practices intertwine with a fast-paced cosmopolitan lifestyle.

Navigating through the bustling streets of Central, exploring the cultural enclaves of Kowloon, or finding solace amidst the lush greenery of Lantau Island, each experience offered a glimpse into the tapestry of Hong Kong's rich tapestry of culture and history.

Yet, beyond its tangible allure, Hong Kong's essence lies in its people—the warmth of locals eager to share their stories, the resilience echoing through the city's past, and the unspoken charm that makes this metropolis an ever-evolving marvel.

This travel guide is a testament to my immersive journey through this captivating city. It's a curated collection of insights, recommendations, and practical tips gleaned from firsthand exploration, aimed to serve as a companion for those seeking to unravel the layers of Hong Kong's splendor. Whether you're a first-time visitor or a seasoned traveler, prepare to embark on an adventure that will ignite your senses and leave an indelible mark on your soul."

OVERVIEW OF HONG KONG

Nestled on the southeastern coast of China, Hong Kong emerges as a dynamic tapestry of culture, commerce, and breathtaking landscapes. This autonomous territory, comprised of Hong Kong Island, Kowloon Peninsula, the New Territories, and a constellation of islands, is a vibrant metropolis that harmoniously intertwines tradition with modernity.

The heartbeat of Hong Kong reverberates through its skyline—a mesmerizing tableau of soaring skyscrapers that silhouette against Victoria Harbour. This juxtaposition of steel and glass against natural beauty encapsulates the essence of this city, where ancient temples sit in the shadows of glittering high-rises, encapsulating a history of adaptation and resilience.

Culture thrives in every corner, from the captivating festivals honoring age-old Chinese traditions to the gastronomic adventures found in every dim sum restaurant or bustling street market. The city's distinct neighborhoods—each with its own character—offer an immersion into diverse experiences, from the financial hub of Central to the lively streets of Tsim Sha Tsui and the eclectic markets of Mong Kok.

Nature's bounty is another facet of Hong Kong's allure, with verdant hillsides, pristine beaches, and hiking trails weaving through its landscape. The Big Buddha perched atop Lantau Island and the panoramic vistas from Victoria Peak showcase just a glimpse of the natural splendor coexisting with the urban bustle.

Hong Kong's magic lies in its ability to fuse tradition with innovation seamlessly. It's a place where history echoes in the streets yet is matched by a futuristic spirit that drives the city forward. Beyond its visual grandeur, Hong Kong is an experience—a tantalizing blend of old-world charm and cutting-edge advancements.

This travel guide is an invitation to explore the depth and diversity of Hong Kong. It's a curated journey through the city's enchanting landmarks, hidden gems, culinary delights, and cultural tapestry—a roadmap designed to ensure that every visitor experiences the pulse of this vibrant city, leaving with a trove of unforgettable memories and a profound appreciation for Hong Kong's rich tapestry of life.

BRIEF HISTORY OF HONG KONG

In the annals of history, Hong Kong's narrative is a compelling tale of transformation, resilience, and cultural convergence. The saga of this bustling metropolis begins centuries ago, evolving from a fishing village into a global powerhouse.

Hong Kong's story intertwines with ancient dynasties, but it was during the Opium Wars in the mid-19th century that its destiny took a pivotal turn. After the First Opium War concluded in 1842, the Treaty of Nanking ceded Hong Kong Island to the British Empire, marking the onset of British colonial rule. Later, in 1860, the Convention of Peking expanded the territory, incorporating the Kowloon Peninsula.

Under British governance, Hong Kong flourished as a strategic trading port. Its deep harbor became a vital hub for international commerce, attracting merchants and traders from around the globe. The city's cosmopolitan character began to take shape, influenced not only by British governance but also by a rich influx of Chinese immigrants seeking opportunities.

The 20th century witnessed Hong Kong's resilience amid adversity. It emerged as a refuge during World War II and later as an economic phoenix after the conflict. The city experienced exponential growth, bolstered by its status as a global financial center and a beacon of free trade.

The transfer of sovereignty from Britain to China in 1997 marked a watershed moment— the creation of the Hong Kong Special Administrative Region (HKSAR). Under the "one country, two systems" principle, Hong Kong retained its distinct legal and economic systems, ensuring a level of autonomy while being part of China.

In recent years, Hong Kong's history has been marked by waves of social and political movements, reflecting the complex interplay between its unique identity and its relationship with mainland China.

Today, as a global financial, cultural, and technological hub, Hong Kong stands as a testament to resilience, innovation, and the harmonious blend of Eastern and Western influences. Its history continues to unfold, adding new chapters to a captivating story of evolution and adaptation.

CULTURE AND TRADITION

Hong Kong's cultural tapestry is a vibrant mosaic woven from a rich heritage of traditions that span centuries, shaped by a fusion of Eastern and Western influences. This dynamic blend manifests itself in the city's festivals, customs, cuisine, and everyday life, creating a captivating and unique cultural identity.

At the heart of Hong Kong's cultural ethos lies a deep reverence for tradition. Festivals such as Chinese New Year, Mid-Autumn Festival, and Dragon Boat Festival are celebrated with fervor, showcasing elaborate rituals, colorful parades, and ancient customs passed down through generations. These festivities not only honor age-old traditions but also serve as a testament to the city's unity and community spirit.

The essence of Hong Kong's cultural fabric is also reflected in its culinary scene. Dim sum, a beloved culinary tradition, symbolizes the art of sharing and enjoying a variety of small, flavorful dishes. From bustling street markets serving up steaming baskets of dumplings to Michelin-starred restaurants crafting exquisite delicacies, food in Hong Kong is an integral part of its cultural heritage.

Beyond festivals and food, the city's architecture, temples, and ancestral halls stand as guardians of tradition. Temples like Wong Tai Sin and Man Mo Temple exude an aura of spirituality and reverence, inviting visitors to immerse themselves in the rituals and beliefs that have endured for centuries.

Hong Kong's cultural landscape is a testament to its resilience, adaptability, and inclusivity, embracing diversity while cherishing its roots. It's a city where ancient customs harmoniously coexist with contemporary trends, creating an immersive experience that unveils the soul of this multifaceted metropolis.

LANGUAGE AND COMMUNICATION

In the bustling streets of Hong Kong, language serves as a colorful tapestry that mirrors the city's diverse heritage and global connectivity. The linguistic landscape of this vibrant metropolis is a fusion of languages, primarily Cantonese, English, and Mandarin, reflecting its unique historical and cultural evolution.

Cantonese, a regional Chinese dialect, stands as the predominant language spoken by the majority of locals. Its melodic tones echo through markets, neighborhoods, and daily interactions, offering visitors a glimpse into the heart of local communication. Learning a few basic Cantonese phrases, such as greetings or expressions of gratitude, often fosters warm connections and appreciation among residents.

Moreover, due to Hong Kong's colonial history, English serves as an official language and is widely used in business, government, education, and tourism. Street signs, menus, and official documents often feature English translations, making navigation and communication accessible for English-speaking visitors.

In recent years, the prevalence of Mandarin has increased, particularly with the influx of mainland Chinese visitors and the city's integration with China. Mandarin is commonly understood in tourist-centric areas, and many locals are bilingual, adding to the linguistic diversity.

The ability to navigate Hong Kong's linguistic maze with basic Cantonese phrases or English can significantly enhance the travel experience, fostering connections and facilitating smoother interactions. However, Hong Kong's multicultural and multilingual environment ensures that communication barriers are often easily bridged, making it a welcoming destination for visitors from around the globe.

2

PLANING YOUR TRIP

BEST TIME TO VISIT

The best time to visit Hong Kong largely hinges on personal preferences and the type of experience desired in this vibrant city. Understanding the distinct seasons and their implications can greatly enhance one's travel experience.

Fall (September to November): This period embodies an ideal climate, characterized by mild temperatures and lower humidity. It's the perfect window for exploration without the crowds. Visitors can enjoy outdoor activities, sightseeing, and cultural experiences comfortably during this time.

Spring (March to May): Similar to fall, spring offers pleasant weather, making it another favorable time to visit. The season is marked by blooming flowers and vibrant foliage, creating picturesque landscapes. It's a fantastic time for outdoor attractions and city exploration.

Summer (June to August): Hong Kong's summers are hot and humid, occasionally accompanied by typhoons. While this season hosts lively festivals like the Dragon Boat Festival and offers fantastic shopping deals during the Hong Kong Summer Sales, the weather might not be conducive to extensive outdoor exploration.

Winter (December to February): Winters in Hong Kong are mild but can occasionally get chilly. The city is adorned with festive decorations during Christmas and Chinese New Year celebrations, offering a unique cultural experience. However, some attractions may experience closures during this time.

Choosing the best time to visit Hong Kong depends on individual preferences regarding weather, crowd levels, and specific events or festivals one might want to experience. Whether it's the pleasant temperatures of fall and spring, the festive atmosphere of winter, or the vibrant energy of summer festivals, Hong Kong welcomes visitors throughout the year with a diverse array of experiences to suit different tastes and interests.

VISA REQUIREMENT

Visa requirements for Hong Kong vary depending on nationality. Many visitors enjoy visa-free entry for durations ranging from 7 to 180 days, making it relatively accessible for tourists from numerous countries. However, some nationalities are required to obtain pre-approved visas before arriving in Hong Kong.

It's essential for travelers to check the specific visa regulations based on their nationality to ensure a smooth entry into the city. The duration of stay permitted under visa-free entry or the requirements for obtaining a visa can differ significantly between countries. Some travelers might be eligible for visa-on-arrival arrangements, while others may need to apply for visas through Hong Kong's immigration authorities before their trip.

Having a clear understanding of the visa requirements and ensuring compliance with the regulations specific to one's nationality is crucial to avoid any travel-related complications. Checking and obtaining the necessary visas in advance ensures a hassle-free entry into Hong Kong, allowing visitors to focus on enjoying the vibrant culture, stunning attractions, and diverse experiences that this cosmopolitan city has to offer.

OCTOPUS CARD

Purchasing an Octopus card is highly recommended for visitors. This reloadable smart card allows seamless access to various modes of transportation and even retail outlets, making traveling within the city hassle-free and cost-effective.

GETTING TO HONG KONG

Getting to Hong Kong is convenient and well-connected, offering various transportation options for travelers from around the world.

By Air: Hong Kong International Airport (HKIA) serves as a major transportation hub, linking the city to numerous international destinations. It provides a seamless travel experience with a wide array of airlines, offering direct flights from various continents. HKIA offers efficient ground transportation options, including taxis, buses, and the Airport Express train, ensuring a smooth transition into the city upon arrival.

By Sea: Ferries operate between Hong Kong and neighboring regions such as Macau and several outlying islands. These ferries offer scenic routes and convenient travel options for those exploring nearby destinations.

By Land: Mainland China is connected to Hong Kong via rail and road networks, providing additional travel options for visitors arriving from or planning to explore other parts of China.

Hong Kong's accessibility by air, sea, and land ensures that travelers have diverse and convenient transportation choices to reach this vibrant city. The well-connected transportation infrastructure offers a seamless transition into Hong Kong, setting the stage for an immersive and memorable travel experience.

TRANSPORTATION WITHIN THE CITY

Navigating within Hong Kong is streamlined by an efficient and comprehensive public transportation system, offering various modes of travel to explore the city's vibrant neighborhoods and attractions.

Mass Transit Railway (MTR): The backbone of Hong Kong's transportation network, the MTR, encompasses trains, light rail, and the high-speed Airport Express. It efficiently connects major tourist spots, business districts, and residential areas. The MTR is known for its cleanliness, reliability, and user-friendly navigation.

For a single trip, the starting price is a mere HK $4.50 (around $0.58), but fares rise according to the distance covered. Opting for a rechargeable Octopus card or a tourist day pass is a smarter move rather than buying separate tickets for every ride. These alternatives are budget-friendly. Acquiring an Octopus card costs HK$50 (approximately $6.40), covering both the card itself and travel until the fare reaches HK-$35. If you return the card before leaving, in good condition with a remaining value below HK$500, the initial HK$50 is refundable. Using an Octopus card sets the base fare at HK$4.40 (about $0.57), but fares increase with longer journeys. Meanwhile, a tourist day pass, priced at HK$55 (about $7) per day, allows unlimited travel across all MTR modes. Trains commence operations at 6 a.m. and wrap up between midnight and 1 a.m., depending on the specific line.

Buses and Trams: Hong Kong's extensive bus network covers areas not serviced by the MTR, providing an economical mode of transport. Trams, an iconic feature of the city, offer a leisurely and nostalgic way to explore Hong Kong Island, offering panoramic views of the surroundings.

Boarding the tram requires either exact change of HK$2.30 (roughly $0.30) or an MTR Octopus card, which offers a flat fare. Additionally, it's important to embark from the rear of the tram.

Ferries: With a harbor as its heart, ferries play a significant role in connecting Hong Kong Island, Kowloon, and the outlying islands. They offer a unique perspective of the city's skyline and a delightful travel experience.

While the Star Ferry remains a favorite among tourists, several other ferry companies ply routes connecting the Kowloon Peninsula, Hong Kong Island, and the outlying islands. For a typical voyage across Victoria Harbour via the Star Ferry, fares range from HK$2 to $3 (under $0.45), contingent on the day, departure point, and arrival pier. To explore further options and details regarding different ferries, the Hong Kong Tourism Board's website offers comprehensive information.

Taxis: Taxis are readily available and offer a convenient means of travel, especially for reaching specific destinations not easily accessible by other modes of transport. However, they can be relatively expensive compared to public transportation. You will be charged HK$27 for the first 2km and HK$1.9 for every 200m.

Hong Kong's diverse transportation options cater to different preferences, ensuring that visitors can explore the city comfortably and efficiently while experiencing its vibrant culture, diverse attractions, and stunning landscapes.

3

ACCOMMODATION

TYPES OF ACCOMMODATION

Hong Kong offers a diverse range of accommodation options to suit various preferences and budgets, ensuring a comfortable stay for every traveler.

Luxury Hotels

The city boasts a plethora of world-class luxury hotels that redefine opulence. From internationally renowned chains to boutique establishments, these hotels offer lavish amenities, stunning harbor views, exquisite dining options, and impeccable service, catering to the discerning traveler seeking luxury and sophistication. Below are some recommended luxury hotels.

Serial	Hotel	Minumum Price ($)	Address
1.	Mandarin Oriental	613	5 Connaught Road Central. +852 2522 0111
2.	The Pier Hotel	112	9 Pak Sha Wan Street, Sai Kung. +852 2912-6777
3.	The Murray, Hong Kong, a Niccolo Hotel	437	22 Cotton Tree Drive, Central. +852 3141 8888
4.	The Pottinger Hong Kong	288	74 Queens Road Central. +852 2308 3188
5.	JW Marriott Hotel	389	88 Queensway. +85228108366
6.	The Fullerton Ocean Park Hotel	203	3 Ocean Drive, Aberdee. +852 2166 7388
7.	Kerry Hotel Hong Kong	307	38 Hung Luen Road, Hung Hom Bay. (852) 2252 5888
8.	The Ritz-Carlton	610	1 Austin Road West, Kowloon. +85222632263
9.	Island Shangri-La	537	Pacific Place, Supreme Court Road, Central. (852) 2877 3838

| 10. | Sheraton Hong Kong Hotel & Towers | 271 | 20 Nathan Road, Kowloon Tsim Sha Tsui. +85223691111 |

Business Hotels

Positioned strategically in central business districts, business hotels provide convenience for corporate travelers. They offer modern facilities, conference rooms, and easy access to commercial hubs, making them ideal for business-related stays. Some recommended business hotels are listed below.

Serial	Hotel	Minumum Price ($)	Address
1.	Mandarin Oriental	613	5 Connaught Road Central. +852 2522 0111
2.	Eaton HK	158	380 Nathan Road Kowloon. (+852) 2782 1818
3.	The Hari Hong Kong	287	330 Lockhart Road, Wan Chai. +852 2129 0388
4.	Prince Hotel	183	23 Canton Road, Harbour City, Tsim Sha Tsui. +852 2113 1888

36

5.	Ibis Hong Kong Central & Sheung Wan	170	Ibis Hong Kong Central & Sheung Wan. +852 2252 2929
6.	The Langham	281	8 Peking Road, Tsim Sha Tsui. (852) 2375 1133
7.	Royal Plaza Hotel	172	193 Prince Edward Road West, Kowloon. (852) 2928 8822
8.	Regal Airport Hotel	169	9 Cheong Tat Road, Hong Kong International Airport, Chek Lap Kok. (852) 2286 88
9.	One-Eight-One Hotel & Serviced Residences	182	181 Connaught Road West. (852) 3181 1688
10.	Sheraton Hong Kong Tung Chung Hotel	207	9 Yi Tung Road, Tung Chung, Lantau Island. +85225350000

Boutique and Design Hotels

Unique boutique and design hotels showcase innovative architecture, stylish interiors, and personalized services. These properties exude character and charm, often reflecting a fusion of contemporary design and local cultural elements.

Budget-Friendly Accommodations

Hong Kong also offers budget-friendly options including hostels, guesthouses, and budget hotels. These accommodations provide comfortable and affordable stays, particularly suitable for backpackers, solo travelers, and those looking to explore the city without breaking the bank. Some recommended budget friendly hotels are listed below.

Serial	Hotel	Minumum Price	Address
1.	Mini Causeway Bay	50	8 Sun Wui Road, Causeway Bay. +852(3427)9490
2.	Ramada Hong Kong Harbour View	58	239 Queen's Road West. +852 25999888

3.	Hotel Ease Mong KOK	63	60 Portland Street. +852 27103688
4.	Ease Tsuen Wan	48	15-19 Chun Pin Street.
5.	Harbour Plaza 8 Degrees	72	199 Kowloon City Road, Tokwawan. +852 21261988
6.	Best Western Plus	70	308 Des Voeux Road West. +852(3)4103333
7.	Best Western Plus	64	73-75 Chatham Road South. +852 23111100
8.	The Cityview	70	23 Waterloo Road. +852(2)7833888
9.	Bishop Lei International House	71	4 Robinson Rd Mid-level.
10.	The Emperor	77	373 Queen's East Road. +852 28933693

Serviced Apartments

Ideal for extended stays or family vacations, serviced apartments offer the comforts of home with amenities such as kitchens, living spaces, and housekeeping services. They provide flexibility and convenience, catering to travelers seeking a more independent and residential experience.

Guesthouses and Homestays
For a more immersive cultural experience, guesthouses and homestays offer the chance to stay with local hosts, providing a glimpse into everyday life in Hong Kong and fostering cultural exchanges.

Hong Kong's diverse accommodation options cater to the varied needs and preferences of travelers, ensuring a memorable and comfortable stay in this bustling metropolis.

POPULAR NEIGHBORHOOD TO STAY IN

Hong Kong showcases a mosaic of neighborhoods, each offering a unique ambiance, attractions, and experiences for travelers seeking accommodation in this vibrant city.

Central: As the heart of Hong Kong's financial district, Central boasts upscale hotels, chic restaurants, and trendy nightlife. It's ideal for business travelers and those seeking luxury accommodations, with easy access to shopping, entertainment, and iconic landmarks like Victoria Peak.

Tsim Sha Tsui: Situated in Kowloon, Tsim Sha Tsui is a bustling neighborhood known for its diverse shopping, dining, and entertainment options. Visitors can find a mix of luxury hotels, budget accommodations, and proximity to attractions like Avenue of Stars, Harbour City Mall, and Victoria Harbour's stunning views.

Mong Kok: Renowned for its vibrant street markets, Mong Kok offers a more local and bustling atmosphere. It's a haven for budget travelers with affordable guesthouses, excellent street food, and a lively night market scene showcasing Hong Kong's local culture.

Causeway Bay: This bustling shopping district is a hub for retail therapy, housing luxury malls, department stores, and vibrant street markets. Visitors can find a range of accommodations, from high-end hotels to more budget-friendly options, along with easy access to Victoria Park and Times Square.

Sheung Wan: Known for its blend of old and new, Sheung Wan exudes a charming vibe with art galleries, antique shops, and trendy cafes. It's perfect for travelers seeking a more laid-back atmosphere while being close to cultural sites like Man Mo Temple and Hollywood Road.

Each neighborhood in Hong Kong offers a distinct flavor, catering to different preferences and interests, ensuring that visitors can find the perfect accommodation and experience the city's diversity firsthand.

4

EXPLORING HONG KONG

TOP ATTRACTIONS

VICTORIA PEAK

Victoria Peak stands as an iconic landmark offering panoramic vistas and a breathtaking perspective of Hong Kong's stunning skyline. This renowned attraction, also known as "The Peak," sits atop the highest point on Hong Kong Island, providing visitors with an unparalleled view that captures the city's vibrant energy.

Traveling to Victoria Peak involves a scenic journey via the historic Peak Tram, a century-old funicular railway that ascends steep slopes, adding an element of adventure to the experience. Upon reaching the summit, visitors are greeted by a viewing platform offering 360-degree views of the city, Victoria Harbour, Kowloon, and the surrounding islands.

The Peak offers more than just panoramic views; it houses shopping malls, restaurants, and entertainment options. The Peak Tower and Peak Galleria feature an array of dining establishments, retail outlets, and attractions, ensuring a delightful experience for visitors exploring this elevated destination.

Apart from daytime vistas, Victoria Peak presents an equally captivating experience at night when the city's skyline comes alive with shimmering lights, creating a mesmerizing panorama. Sunset or evening visits to The Peak offer a spectacular view as the city transitions from day to night, illuminating the harbor and skyscrapers in a dazzling display.

Victoria Peak remains an essential stop for tourists, promising unparalleled vistas and a memorable experience that captures the essence of Hong Kong's captivating skyline and dynamic energy.

HONG KONG DISNEYLAND

Hong Kong Disneyland stands as a magical destination where fantasy comes to life, offering an enchanting experience for visitors of all ages. This iconic theme park, nestled on Lantau Island, invites guests into a world of imagination, adventure, and beloved Disney characters.

The park's distinct zones, like Main Street, U.S.A., Adventureland, Fantasyland, Tomorrowland, and Toy Story Land, offer a diverse array of attractions and entertainment, each meticulously designed to immerse guests in the wonder of Disney magic. From thrilling rides like Space Mountain and Big Grizzly Mountain Runaway Mine Cars to enchanting experiences such as meeting iconic characters and enjoying spectacular parades, the park promises a journey of excitement and nostalgia.

Hong Kong Disneyland's unique cultural blend infuses traditional Chinese elements into its entertainment, showcasing a fusion of Disney magic and local flair. The park hosts seasonal events, special performances, and fireworks displays that captivate visitors year-round, making each visit a memorable and immersive experience.

With its captivating attractions, live entertainment, themed dining, and magical ambiance, Hong Kong Disneyland offers a whimsical escape, creating cherished memories for families, Disney enthusiasts, and anyone seeking to relive the enchantment of their favorite childhood stories in a captivating setting.

TIAN TAN BUDDHA

Nestled serenely on Lantau Island, the Tian Tan Buddha stands as an awe-inspiring symbol of spirituality and tranquility in Hong Kong. Also known as the Big Buddha, this majestic bronze statue is a revered icon and a significant Buddhist pilgrimage site.

Ascending to the Tian Tan Buddha involves a journey of reverence and wonder. Visitors can ascend via a breathtaking 268-step staircase or opt for the Ngong Ping 360 cable car, offering panoramic views of the island's lush landscapes and the South China Sea.

At 112 feet tall, the Tian Tan Buddha presides over the Po Lin Monastery, exuding a sense of serenity and grandeur. The statue's intricate craftsmanship and serene countenance captivate visitors, offering a moment of contemplation and spiritual reflection.

Surrounded by scenic vistas and mountainous terrain, the site invites exploration beyond the statue itself. The Ngong Ping Village nearby offers cultural experiences, tea houses, and vegetarian dining options, providing visitors with a deeper understanding of Buddhist traditions and a tranquil escape from the city's hustle.

Tian Tan Buddha stands as a testament to Hong Kong's cultural heritage and spiritual significance, offering a profound and unforgettable experience for travelers seeking tranquility and spiritual connection amidst the city's vibrant energy.

AVENUE OF STARS

The Avenue of Stars, nestled along the glittering Victoria Harbour in Tsim Sha Tsui, pays homage to Hong Kong's vibrant film industry and celebrates the stars who have contributed to its cinematic legacy. This waterfront promenade offers a captivating blend of stunning views, interactive exhibits, and tributes to legendary film icons.

Featuring handprints, sculptures, and information plaques, the Avenue of Stars immortalizes the contributions of Hong Kong's movie legends, such as Bruce Lee and Jackie Chan. Visitors can stroll along the harborfront, relishing the panoramic views of Hong Kong Island's skyline while discovering the footprints and signatures of beloved stars set in the pavement.

The "Symphony of Stars" light and sound show illuminates the evenings, captivating audiences with an enchanting display of music, lights, and projections on the harbor's skyline, creating a captivating spectacle that celebrates the city's cinematic history.

Recently redeveloped, the Avenue of Stars also includes interactive installations, storytelling panels, and multimedia exhibits that offer insights into the city's film industry, making it an engaging and educational experience for visitors interested in Hong Kong's cinematic heritage.

The Avenue of Stars stands as a vibrant tribute to the stars of Hong Kong cinema, providing a scenic and culturally enriching experience along Victoria Harbour, making it a must-visit destination for film enthusiasts and travelers exploring Tsim Sha Tsui.

OCEAN PARK

Ocean Park, perched on the southern coast of Hong Kong Island, stands as a thrilling amalgamation of entertainment, conservation, and marine exploration. This iconic theme park offers a world of excitement and educational experiences for visitors of all ages.

Divided into two main areas, the Waterfront and the Summit, Ocean Park presents a diverse range of attractions and adventures. The Waterfront hosts thrilling rides, animal exhibits, and vibrant shows, providing a perfect blend of entertainment and conservation awareness. The Grand Aquarium, home to an array of marine life, and the adventurous roller coasters like the Hair Raiser and The Rapids immerse visitors in exhilarating experiences.

The Summit, accessible via a scenic cable car ride or a picturesque funicular train, offers panoramic views of the South China Sea and boasts attractions like the Polar Adventure, Rainforest, and Thrill Mountain. These zones feature habitats showcasing animals from various regions, interactive exhibits, and adrenaline-pumping rides, offering a perfect mix of adventure and education.

Beyond the entertainment, Ocean Park is committed to marine conservation and education, engaging visitors through conservation programs, animal encounters, and immersive experiences that foster an appreciation for wildlife and environmental preservation.

Ocean Park stands as a quintessential destination, blending entertainment, education, and conservation efforts, making it an engaging and unforgettable experience for families, thrill-seekers, and nature enthusiasts visiting Hong Kong.

NGONG PING 360

Ngong Ping 360, an iconic attraction on Lantau Island, offers a breathtaking journey and cultural immersion through its cable car ride and cultural village experience. This immersive destination combines stunning natural vistas with cultural insights, providing visitors with a memorable experience.

The Ngong Ping Cable Car ride is the highlight, offering panoramic views of Lantau Island's picturesque landscapes, the sparkling South China Sea, and the lush greenery below. The journey spans across 5.7 kilometers, taking guests on a scenic ride over the island's hills and forests, offering unparalleled views of the Tian Tan Buddha and the serene Ngong Ping Plateau.

Upon arrival at Ngong Ping Village, visitors encounter a cultural oasis. The village features traditional architecture, charming tea houses, and souvenir shops, providing a glimpse into Hong Kong's rich heritage. The Po Lin Monastery, nestled nearby, adds to the spiritual ambiance, inviting guests to explore its serene halls and tranquil surroundings.

The cultural village offers diverse experiences, including cultural shows, workshops, and encounters with local artisans, immersing visitors in the traditions and customs of Hong Kong's cultural tapestry.

Ngong Ping 360 serves as a gateway to both natural beauty and cultural heritage, offering an enriching experience that captures the essence of Lantau Island's beauty and spiritual significance, making it a must-visit destination for travelers seeking serenity and cultural exploration.

5

DISTRICTS AND

NEIGHBORHOODS

TSIM SHA TSUI

Tsim Sha Tsui, situated in the vibrant Kowloon district, stands as a bustling hub of culture, shopping, and entertainment, offering an eclectic mix of attractions and experiences for visitors to Hong Kong.

The district pulsates with energy, boasting an array of shopping centers, luxury boutiques, and local markets. Visitors can explore the upscale Harbor City mall, stroll along Nathan Road—Kowloon's main thoroughfare—lined with shops and restaurants, or immerse themselves in the bustling markets of Temple Street Night Market and Jade Market, offering a treasure trove of souvenirs, antiques, and local delicacies.

Tsim Sha Tsui's waterfront promenade offers mesmerizing views of Hong Kong Island's iconic skyline and Victoria Harbour. The Avenue of Stars, a tribute to the city's film industry, features handprints of movie stars and offers a scenic walk along the harbor.

Cultural enthusiasts can explore the Hong Kong Space Museum, Hong Kong Museum of Art, or indulge in a performance at the Hong Kong Cultural Centre, offering a diverse array of artistic and cultural experiences.

The district also boasts an array of dining options, from street-side stalls serving local favorites to Michelin-starred restaurants, ensuring a culinary adventure for every palate.

Tsim Sha Tsui's vibrant ambiance, cultural richness, and diverse attractions make it a dynamic and bustling destination, catering to shoppers, culture enthusiasts, and those seeking a vibrant urban experience in Hong Kong.

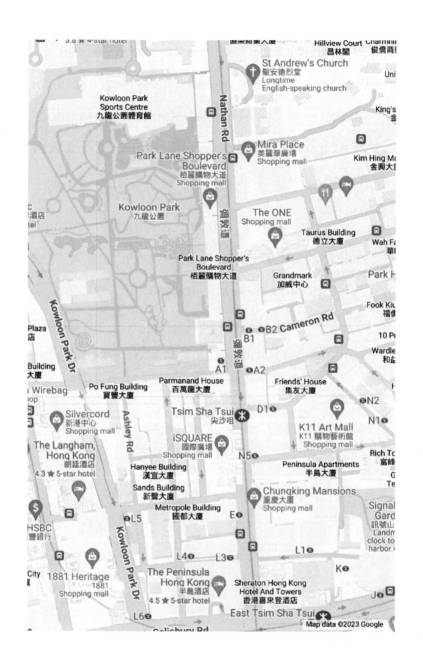

CENTRAL

Central, a dynamic district in the heart of Hong Kong, stands as the city's financial and commercial hub, pulsating with energy, culture, and history. This bustling neighborhood seamlessly blends modern skyscrapers with colonial architecture, offering a fascinating juxtaposition of the old and new.

The district hosts an array of upscale boutiques, designer stores, and luxury malls like The Landmark and IFC Mall, catering to sophisticated shoppers. It also boasts an eclectic dining scene, from Michelin-starred restaurants to trendy cafes and local eateries, showcasing diverse culinary delights.

Central is home to numerous landmarks, including Statue Square, where locals and visitors converge, and the historic Man Mo Temple, steeped in tradition and spirituality. The iconic Hong Kong Zoological and Botanical Gardens offer a serene retreat amidst the urban landscape.

The neighborhood is easily navigable via the efficient Mass Transit Railway (MTR) network and the iconic Central-Mid-Levels Escalator, the world's longest outdoor covered escalator system, offering convenient access to nearby areas like SoHo (South of Hollywood Road) known for its vibrant nightlife and dining scene.

With its blend of commerce, culture, and historic landmarks, Central embodies the essence of Hong Kong's cosmopolitan spirit, making it a vibrant destination for business, leisure, and cultural exploration.

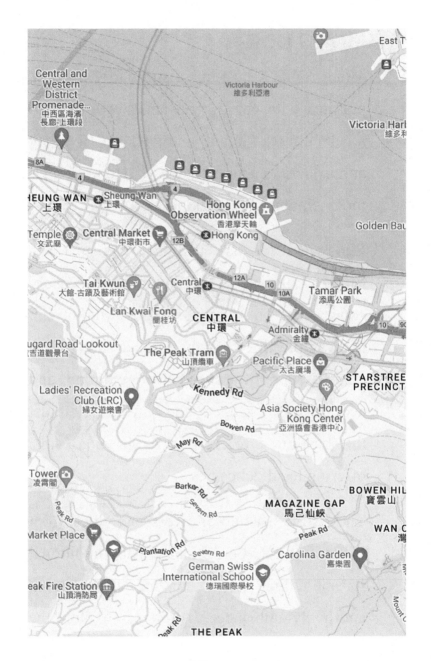

MONG KOK

Mong Kok, a bustling district in Kowloon, pulsates with energy and an eclectic mix of local culture, vibrant markets, and a lively atmosphere, making it one of Hong Kong's most vibrant neighborhoods.

Renowned for its bustling street markets, Mong Kok offers an immersive sensory experience. The famous Ladies' Market and the Temple Street Night Market showcase a kaleidoscope of goods, from clothing and accessories to gadgets and souvenirs, amidst the bustling streets lined with food stalls offering local delicacies.

The district is a hub of diverse activities, from vibrant street performances to traditional fortune-telling stalls, creating an engaging and lively ambiance. Visitors can explore the

Mong Kok Computer Centre for tech gadgets or wander through the Sneaker Street, a haven for sneaker enthusiasts.

Mong Kok is also a gastronomic delight, with an array of street food stalls and local eateries offering an eclectic mix of culinary treats, including fish balls, egg waffles, and dai pai dongs (open-air food stalls), allowing visitors to savor authentic flavors of Hong Kong.

The neighborhood's vibrant energy, cultural richness, and diverse offerings make Mong Kok a must-visit destination for travelers seeking an immersive and lively experience, capturing the essence of Hong Kong's local life and dynamic street culture.

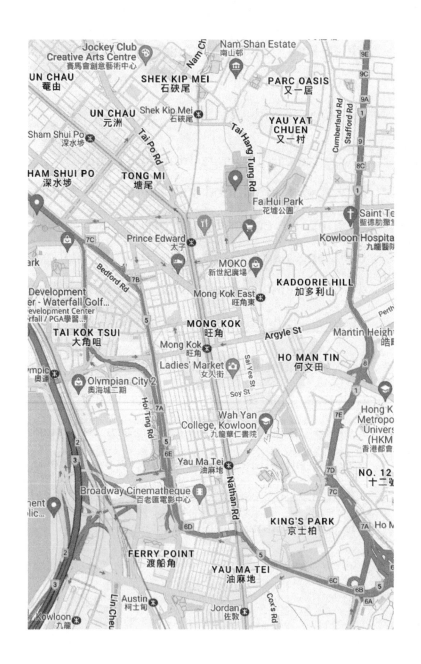

CAUSEWAY BAY

Causeway Bay, a bustling district on Hong Kong Island, epitomizes the city's vibrant urban lifestyle, offering a blend of high-end shopping, entertainment, and cultural experiences.

The area is renowned for its shopping prowess, boasting an array of luxury malls like Times Square, Hysan Place, and Lee Gardens, showcasing global brands, designer labels, and trendy boutiques. Visitors can indulge in retail therapy, explore the latest fashion trends, and enjoy an immersive shopping experience.

Causeway Bay is a culinary haven, featuring a diverse range of dining options, from upscale restaurants serving international cuisine to local cha chaan tengs (tea restaurants) offering authentic Hong Kong fare. Visitors can savor a variety of culinary delights, including dim sum, seafood, and delectable street food.

Beyond shopping and dining, the district is bustling with cultural attractions and entertainment. The Victoria Park provides a green oasis in the midst of the urban landscape, while the Hong Kong Central Library offers a serene environment for book lovers.

The district's dynamic energy, shopping allure, diverse dining scene, and cultural offerings make Causeway Bay an exciting destination for visitors seeking a blend of modernity, culture, and entertainment in the heart of Hong Kong.

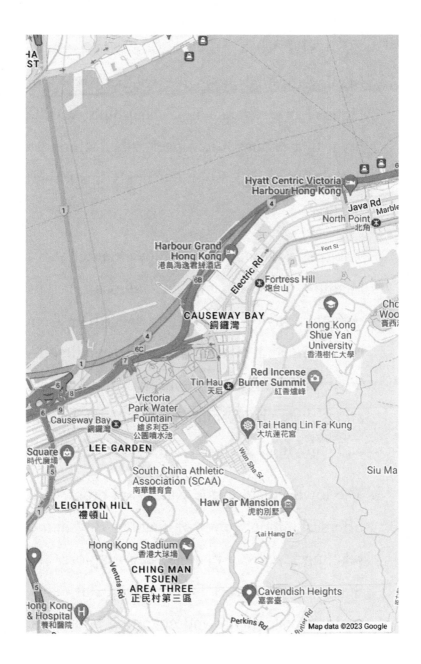

STANLEY

Stanley, nestled along the southern coast of Hong Kong Island, is a charming seaside town that exudes a laid-back vibe, offering a delightful escape from the city's hustle and bustle.

The main attraction, Stanley Market, is a bustling open-air market famous for its eclectic array of stalls selling everything from souvenirs and clothing to local handicrafts. Visitors can immerse themselves in the lively atmosphere, bargaining for unique treasures and enjoying the vibrant ambiance.

The town's picturesque waterfront promenade offers stunning views of Stanley Bay and a relaxing escape. Visitors can explore the Stanley Main Street lined with quaint cafes, seafood restaurants, and charming boutiques, perfect for leisurely strolls and alfresco dining.

Stanley is also home to historic landmarks like Murray House, a colonial-era building relocated from Central, now housing restaurants and shops, and Tin Hau Temple, a cultural gem dedicated to the goddess of the sea.

The laid-back coastal ambiance, vibrant market scene, scenic promenade, and cultural landmarks make Stanley a popular destination for locals and tourists alike, offering a refreshing contrast to the city's urban landscape and a relaxing getaway on Hong Kong Island's southern shores.

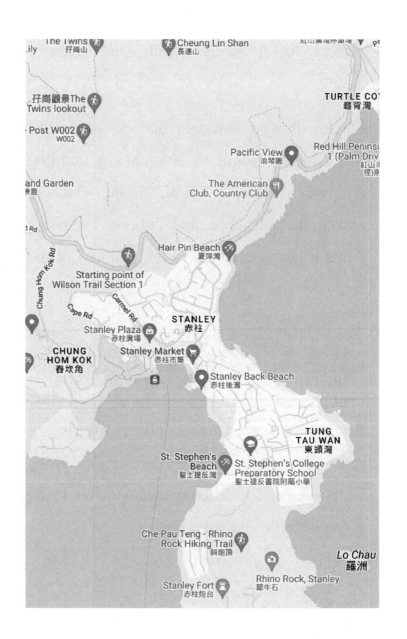

6

CULTURAL

EXPERIENCES

TRADITIONAL MARKET

Traditional markets in Hong Kong offer an authentic glimpse into the city's vibrant culture, bustling energy, and rich heritage. These markets are immersive experiences, showcasing local life, culinary delights, and a treasure trove of goods.

The bustling Mong Kok Ladies' Market and Temple Street Night Market in Yau Ma Tei are renowned for their vibrant atmosphere and diverse offerings. Visitors can explore stalls selling everything from clothing, accessories, and electronics to antiques, souvenirs, and local artworks. These markets engage all senses, with street food aromas wafting through the air, vibrant colors, and the lively banter of vendors and shoppers.

Wet markets, like the Central Market and Wan Chai Market, are cultural hubs offering fresh produce, seafood, and meats. These markets provide an authentic glimpse into daily life as locals shop for groceries, and visitors can witness the vibrant array of ingredients used in Hong Kong's culinary scene.

For a taste of tradition, the Sheung Wan Dried Seafood Street and Tai Yuen Street Market in Wan Chai offer a glimpse into Hong Kong's heritage, showcasing traditional dried seafood, herbs, and Chinese preserved goods.

These traditional markets are not just shopping destinations but cultural experiences, offering a captivating journey into Hong Kong's local life, culinary heritage, and the city's vibrant tapestry of sights, sounds, and flavors.

WONG TAI SIN TEMPLE

Wong Tai Sin Temple, a revered Taoist shrine nestled in Kowloon, stands as a spiritual sanctuary and a testament to faith, attracting locals and tourists seeking blessings, fortune telling, and spiritual guidance.

Dedicated to the Taoist deity Wong Tai Sin, worshipped for granting wishes and answering prayers, the temple exudes a serene ambiance amidst its bustling surroundings. The complex is adorned with vibrant red pillars, intricate roofs, and traditional Chinese architectural elements, creating an atmosphere steeped in cultural richness and spirituality.

Visitors flock to Wong Tai Sin Temple to seek blessings and guidance by offering incense, making offerings, and practicing traditional rituals. Fortune tellers and palm readers stationed around the temple offer insights and predictions, adding to the mystical allure of the site.

The temple's Hall of Three Saints, Good Wish Garden, and the Nine Dragons Wall are among the notable features that showcase the intricate craftsmanship and spiritual significance within the complex.

The temple also hosts various festivals, including the colorful celebrations during the Wong Tai Sin Festival, attracting devotees and spectators to partake in the vibrant festivities and cultural performances.

Wong Tai Sin Temple stands as a revered sanctuary, offering a spiritual haven and a cultural experience, allowing visitors to immerse themselves in Hong Kong's rich religious heritage and seek blessings for health, prosperity, and good fortune.

CHI LIN NUNNERY

The Chi Lin Nunnery, an oasis of tranquility nestled amidst the urban landscape of Kowloon, stands as a harmonious blend of traditional Tang Dynasty architecture and serene Buddhist spirituality.

Constructed entirely without the use of nails, this elegant complex showcases classical Chinese architecture, featuring intricate wooden carvings, tranquil lotus ponds, meticulously landscaped gardens, and traditional timber structures. The architecture and serene environment create a serene ambiance conducive to meditation and contemplation.

The nunnery serves as a Buddhist sanctuary and a haven for spiritual seekers. Visitors can explore the halls adorned with Buddhist scriptures and statues, offering insights into Buddhist teachings and rituals. The serene lotus ponds and meticulously maintained gardens provide a peaceful respite from the city's hustle.

Adjacent to the nunnery is the Nan Lian Garden, a meticulously landscaped classical Chinese garden. This lush oasis features winding pathways, bonsai trees, ornamental rocks, and traditional Tang-style architecture, offering a picturesque escape for visitors seeking tranquility.

The Chi Lin Nunnery and Nan Lian Garden stand as cultural gems, offering a serene retreat and a glimpse into traditional Chinese architecture, landscaping, and Buddhist spirituality amidst the bustling urban landscape of Hong Kong.

TEA HOUSES AND DIM SUM CULTURE

Hong Kong's tea houses and dim sum culture are integral parts of the city's culinary heritage, offering a flavorful journey into local tastes and traditions.

Tea houses, known as "cha chaan tengs," are iconic establishments that epitomize Hong Kong's dining culture. These bustling eateries serve a fusion of Chinese and Western cuisines, offering a diverse menu of comfort food. Visitors can savor aromatic Hong Kong-style milk tea, crispy pineapple buns, egg tarts, and other signature delights, all served amidst a lively atmosphere buzzing with locals and tourists.

Dim sum, small savory and sweet delicacies served in bamboo steamers or on small plates, is a quintessential part of Hong Kong's dining experience. Dim sum restaurants are vibrant hubs where families and friends gather to enjoy an assortment of dumplings, buns, and pastries. Visitors can indulge in a variety of dim sum classics, such as har gow (shrimp dumplings), siu mai (pork dumplings), and char siu bao (barbecue pork buns), experiencing the rich flavors and culinary craftsmanship.

These culinary experiences offer more than just delectable dishes; they embody Hong Kong's vibrant dining culture, providing a glimpse into the city's diverse culinary heritage and the art of communal dining and tea appreciation that has been cherished for generations.

HONG KONG MUSEUM OF HISTORY

The Hong Kong Museum of History stands as a captivating journey through the city's rich and diverse heritage, offering visitors a comprehensive exploration of Hong Kong's history, culture, and traditions.

Spanning thousands of years, the museum's exhibits chronicle the region's evolution, from its prehistoric beginnings to the modern metropolis it is today. Visitors embark on an immersive experience, encountering artifacts, multimedia displays, and lifelike dioramas that vividly depict Hong Kong's historical milestones, including its maritime history, colonial era, and the city's transformation into a global financial hub.

The museum's permanent exhibitions cover a wide array of topics, including archaeology, ethnography, natural history, and the city's social and economic development. Notable displays include reconstructed scenes of ancient villages, interactive exhibits showcasing traditional Chinese festivals, and insightful portrayals of Hong Kong's role during significant historical events.

The museum also hosts temporary exhibitions and educational programs that delve deeper into various aspects of Hong Kong's past, offering visitors an ever-evolving and enriching experience.

The Hong Kong Museum of History serves as a cultural treasure trove, providing a captivating and educational journey that invites visitors to explore and appreciate the diverse tapestry of Hong Kong's history and cultural heritage.

7

OUTDOOR ADVENTURES

HIKING TRAILS (DRAGON'S BACK, LANTAU PEAK)

Hong Kong's hiking trails offer outdoor enthusiasts and nature lovers a chance to explore the city's breathtaking landscapes and scenic vistas. Among these, the Dragon's Back and Lantau Peak trails stand out as iconic routes, providing unforgettable experiences amidst stunning natural beauty.

The Dragon's Back trail, named for its undulating path resembling a dragon's spine, offers panoramic views of Hong Kong's coastline, lush forests, and stunning vistas of the South China Sea. This moderately challenging trail, easily accessible from the city, meanders through Shek O Country Park, offering hikers a perfect blend of nature and coastal scenery.

Lantau Peak, the second-highest peak in Hong Kong, boasts a challenging yet rewarding hiking experience. The trail leads through picturesque landscapes, ancient monasteries, and dense forests before ascending to the summit. Hikers are rewarded with awe-inspiring views of the surrounding islands, including the iconic Tian Tan Buddha, and a stunning sunrise or sunset depending on the chosen hike time.

Both trails showcase Hong Kong's diverse natural beauty, offering a chance to escape the urban bustle and immerse oneself in serene landscapes and captivating views. Whether seeking adventure or a serene retreat, these trails provide an unforgettable outdoor experience in Hong Kong's scenic wilderness.

BEACHES

Hong Kong's beaches, such as Repulse Bay and Shek O, offer scenic coastal retreats that beckon locals and tourists alike, providing a tranquil escape from the city's urban hustle.

Repulse Bay, with its crescent-shaped shoreline, stands as one of Hong Kong's most popular and picturesque beaches. Framed by high-rise apartments and lush hills, this beach exudes a relaxed ambiance and offers golden sands, azure waters, and facilities for sunbathing, swimming, and water sports. Visitors can also explore the adjacent temples, upscale restaurants, and the iconic statue of Kwun Yam, the Goddess of Mercy.

Shek O Beach, nestled along the southeastern coast, charms visitors with its pristine shores, rocky outcrops, and clear waters. It caters to both beach enthusiasts and thrill-seekers, offering opportunities for sunbathing, swimming, and beach volleyball, as well as water sports like surfing and kayaking. The laid-back atmosphere, scenic landscapes, and beachside eateries add to the charm of this coastal gem.

Both Repulse Bay and Shek O embody Hong Kong's natural beauty, providing idyllic settings for relaxation, recreation, and unwinding amidst stunning coastal scenery, making them popular destinations for locals and tourists seeking a coastal retreat in the vibrant city.

HARBOUR CRUISES

Harbour cruises in Hong Kong offer a captivating way to experience the city's stunning skyline, vibrant harbor, and iconic landmarks from a unique vantage point.

These cruises traverse the renowned Victoria Harbour, allowing passengers to witness the mesmerizing cityscape that juxtaposes modern skyscrapers with historic landmarks. As the cruise glides along the water, visitors are treated to panoramic views of architectural marvels like the towering International Commerce Centre, the Hong Kong Convention and Exhibition Centre, and the iconic Symphony of Lights illuminating the skyline.

Harbour cruises come in various forms, from leisurely sightseeing journeys aboard traditional Chinese junk boats to luxurious dinner cruises with gourmet meals and live entertainment. Some cruises also offer informative commentary, providing insights into Hong Kong's history, culture, and the significance of the landmarks that dot the harbor.

The Symphony of Lights, a multimedia light and laser show synchronizing music and lights across the harbor's buildings, is a highlight of these cruises, creating a dazzling spectacle best witnessed from the water.

Harbour cruises in Hong Kong offer an unforgettable experience, allowing visitors to appreciate the city's beauty, dynamism, and cultural richness while gliding through the shimmering waters of Victoria Harbour, making it a must-do activity for travelers seeking a unique perspective of this vibrant metropolis.

TAI O FISHING VILLAGE

Tai O Fishing Village, nestled on the western coast of Lantau Island, stands as a picturesque and culturally rich enclave, offering a glimpse into Hong Kong's traditional fishing heritage.

Famed for its stilt houses, the village presents a captivating scene of homes built on wooden stilts above the tidal flats, creating a unique waterfront setting. Visitors can explore the narrow lanes flanked by traditional shops selling dried seafood, local snacks, and souvenirs, immersing themselves in the village's rustic charm.

The village's cultural significance is exemplified by the Tanka people, the indigenous community renowned for their fishing expertise and their traditional lifestyle. Travelers can engage with the locals, learn about their fishing techniques, and even embark on boat tours to witness the unique stilt-house architecture and the village's serene waterways.

Beyond its rustic allure, Tai O offers nature enthusiasts the opportunity to explore the nearby Tai O Heritage Hotel, once a police station, and the nearby Tai O Infinity Pool, offering panoramic views of the surrounding landscapes.

Tai O Fishing Village stands as a testament to Hong Kong's maritime heritage, offering a blend of cultural immersion, picturesque scenery, and insights into the traditional ways of life that have endured for generations, making it a captivating destination for visitors seeking a glimpse into the city's storied past.

8

FOOD AND DINING

MUST-TRY LOCAL DISHES

Hong Kong's culinary landscape is a vibrant fusion of traditional Chinese flavors and global influences, offering a diverse array of must-try dishes that captivate taste buds and showcase the city's rich food culture.

Dim Sum

Dim sum is a quintessential Hong Kong dining experience, comprising an assortment of small, flavorful dishes served in bamboo steamers or on small plates. From delicate dumplings like har gow (shrimp dumplings) and siu mai (pork dumplings) to fluffy char siu bao (barbecue pork buns) and crispy spring rolls, dim sum restaurants offer a delightful variety of flavors and textures.

Roast Meats

Hong Kong's roast meats, prepared with expert precision, are a gastronomic delight. Succulent roast duck with crispy skin, tender char siu (barbecue pork), and juicy siu yuk (roast pork belly) are among the favorites. Served with rice or noodles and accompanied by flavorful sauces, these meats showcase the city's culinary mastery.

Egg Waffles (Gai Daan Jai)

Egg waffles are a beloved street snack with a delightful crispy exterior and a soft, fluffy interior. The batter is poured into a distinctive honeycomb-shaped mold, resulting in a treat that's both visually appealing and deliciously satisfying.

Hong Kong-style Milk Tea

This iconic beverage is a blend of strong black tea and evaporated or condensed milk, strained through a cloth filter. Known for its robust flavor and silky smoothness, Hong Kong-style milk tea is a staple in local cha chaan tengs (tea restaurants) and offers a comforting refreshment.

Wonton Noodle Soup

Featuring springy egg noodles served in a clear, flavorful broth with plump wontons filled with minced meat, wonton noodle soup is a classic comfort dish. Often accompanied by leafy greens, this dish is simple yet incredibly satisfying.

Pineapple Bun (Bo Lo Bao)

The pineapple bun, despite its name, doesn't contain pineapple but derives its name from the sugary, crispy crust resembling a pineapple's texture. Inside, it's soft and fluffy, making it a popular breakfast or snack choice.

Clay Pot Rice

Clay pot rice is a comforting dish where rice is cooked with various toppings like Chinese sausage, chicken, or vegetables in a clay pot, creating a flavorful one-pot meal. The rice at the bottom becomes crispy, adding depth to the dish.

Steamed Fish

Fresh fish, usually grouper or sea bass, is steamed to perfection with ginger, scallions, and soy sauce, retaining its delicate flavors and tenderness. This dish exemplifies the Chinese culinary technique of cooking seafood with minimal seasoning to highlight its natural taste.

Exploring these dishes is an adventure in itself, whether in local eateries, street food stalls, or upscale restaurants. These culinary delights epitomize Hong Kong's diverse food culture, showcasing a fusion of flavors and culinary traditions that have been cherished for generations. The city's vibrant dining scene invites visitors to savor these iconic dishes while experiencing the essence of Hong Kong's rich gastronomic heritage.

MICHELIN-STARRED RESTAURANTS

Hong Kong boasts a constellation of Michelin-starred restaurants, offering discerning diners an exquisite culinary journey that reflects the city's gastronomic excellence and diverse culinary landscape.

Bo Innovation

This pioneering restaurant infuses traditional Cantonese cuisine with modern flair, creating innovative and visually stunning dishes. Chef Alvin Leung's daring and imaginative approach has earned Bo Innovation its Michelin stars.

1/F, H Code, 45 Pottinger St,

Central.

+852 2850 8371

www.boinnovation.com

The Chairman

Known for its commitment to using premium local ingredients, The Chairman offers authentic Cantonese cuisine with a focus on traditional flavors and heritage recipes. Dishes like steamed crab claw with aged Shaoxing wine and braised spare ribs exemplify the restaurant's dedication to craftsmanship.

The Wellington (3rd Floor,)

198 Wellington St,

Central

+852 2555 2202

www.thechairmangroup.com

L'Atelier de Joël Robuchon

Led by the late Chef Joël Robuchon, this sophisticated French restaurant offers an interactive dining experience with its open kitchen concept. Patrons can savor exquisite French cuisine like the famous mashed potatoes and innovative tasting menus.

Shop 401, Landmark Atrium,

15 Queen's Road Central, Central.

+852 2166 9000

www.robuchon.hk

Sushi Shikon

This intimate sushi restaurant, led by Master Chef Masahiro Yoshitake, specializes in Edomae sushi—sushi made using traditional Tokyo-style techniques. With its focus on seasonal ingredients and precise craftsmanship, it offers an authentic Japanese culinary experience.

The Landmark, 15 Queen's Road Central, Central,

+852 2643 6800

www.sushi-shikon.com

Amber

Located within The Landmark Mandarin Oriental, Amber offers contemporary French cuisine under the direction of Chef Richard

Ekkebus. Known for its innovative dishes and impeccable service, the restaurant's tasting menus delight diners with creative flavors and presentations.

15 Queen's Road Central,

Central.

+852 2132 0066

www.mandarinoriental.com

T'ang Court

This Cantonese restaurant at The Langham, Hong Kong, has retained its three Michelin stars by offering exquisite and refined Cantonese dishes. Its dedication to culinary excellence and impeccable service makes it a standout dining destination.

These Michelin-starred restaurants showcase the diverse culinary talents in Hong Kong, spanning a range of cuisines and styles. Each establishment offers a unique gastronomic experience, reflecting the city's reputation as a global culinary hotspot and inviting diners to indulge in world-class cuisine within the vibrant streets of Hong Kong.

1F and 2F, The Langham,

8 Peking Rd, Tsim Sha Tsui.

+852 2132 7898

www.langhamhotels.com

Street Food Culture

Hong Kong's street food culture is a vibrant tapestry of flavors, aromas, and culinary traditions that thrive in bustling markets and vibrant street corners, offering an authentic and delicious taste of the city's diverse gastronomy.

Stalls and Markets

Throughout the city, bustling street markets like Temple Street Night Market, Ladies' Market in Mong Kok, and Sham Shui Po's food stalls present a colorful array of local delicacies. From sizzling skewers of curry fish balls and fragrant egg waffles to aromatic stews and noodle soups, these stalls offer a sensory feast for locals and tourists alike.

Local Favorites

Signature street food items such as siu mai (steamed pork dumplings), cheung fun (rice noodle rolls), egg tarts, and pineapple buns delight taste buds with their diverse flavors and textures. The aroma of freshly steamed dim sum, the sizzle of grilling skewers, and the hustle of vendors create an exciting and immersive street food experience.

Cultural Experience

Beyond the culinary delights, street food in Hong Kong embodies a vibrant cultural experience. It's a place where locals gather to socialize, share stories, and indulge in beloved dishes passed down through generations. Visitors can engage with vendors, observe the art of preparation, and savor authentic flavors while experiencing the city's dynamic street life.

Hong Kong's street food culture is a celebration of culinary craftsmanship, cultural heritage, and bustling energy, inviting travelers to explore its vibrant streets and indulge in a flavorful and authentic culinary adventure.

9

SHOPPING IN HONG KONG

LUXURY SHOPPING MALLS

Hong Kong stands as a global hub for luxury shopping, offering an array of opulent malls that redefine the concept of upscale retail therapy amidst the city's cosmopolitan atmosphere.

The Landmark

Nestled in Central, The Landmark is a premier luxury shopping destination housing a curated selection of high-end fashion brands like Louis Vuitton, Gucci, and Chanel. With its exclusive boutiques and elegant ambiance, it caters to sophisticated shoppers seeking designer labels and exquisite craftsmanship.

5 Queen's Road Central,

Central.

+852 2500 0555

www.landmark.hk

Pacific Place

Located in Admiralty, Pacific Place is an upscale mall that features a blend of luxury fashion, lifestyle brands, and fine dining establishments. From iconic fashion houses to exclusive beauty boutiques, it offers a refined shopping experience.

88 Queensway,

Admiralty.

+852 2844 8988

www.pacificplace.com.hk

Harbour City

Situated in Tsim Sha Tsui, Harbour City is one of the largest and most diverse shopping complexes in Hong Kong, encompassing luxury brands, designer boutiques, and flagship stores. Its expansive layout houses prestigious labels like Hermès, Dior, and Prada, catering to discerning shoppers.

Canton Rd, Tsim Sha Tsui

+852 2118 8666

www.harbourcity.com.hk

Elements

In West Kowloon, Elements boasts a modern and stylish setting with an impressive lineup of luxury retailers, including renowned fashion houses, jewelry boutiques, and lifestyle brands. It combines shopping with dining and entertainment, providing a comprehensive luxury shopping experience.

These luxury malls not only offer an unparalleled selection of high-end brands but also create an immersive shopping journey, replete with elegant interiors, exclusive services, and a sophisticated ambiance that caters to the discerning tastes of luxury shoppers in Hong Kong.

1 Austin Rd W,

Tsim Sha Tsui

www.elementshk.com

MARKETS FOR BARGAIN HUNTING

Hong Kong's markets are treasure troves for bargain hunters, offering an eclectic array of goods, souvenirs, and unique finds at wallet-friendly prices, making them essential destinations for savvy shoppers.

Ladies' Market

This bustling market in Mong Kok spans over a kilometer, offering a vibrant assortment of clothing, accessories, and knick-knacks. Bargaining is part of the experience here, allowing visitors to snag great deals on trendy fashion items, accessories, and souvenirs.

Temple Street Night Market

Known for its lively atmosphere, this market in Yau Ma Tei comes alive in the evenings, offering a diverse range of goods, from trinkets and antiques to electronics and local street food. Visitors can haggle with vendors for items like clothing, jade, and gadgets.

Stanley Market

Nestled in the charming seaside town of Stanley, this market boasts a relaxed ambiance and offers a mix of stalls selling art, souvenirs, clothing, and home decor. Visitors can find unique gifts and artwork while enjoying the laid-back vibe of the waterfront area.

Apliu Street Flea Market

Tech enthusiasts and bargain hunters flock to this market in Sham Shui Po, specializing in electronics, gadgets, and second-hand goods. From vintage cameras to electronic components, it's a haven for tech finds at affordable prices.

Navigating these markets offers not just the thrill of bargain hunting but also a glimpse into Hong Kong's vibrant street life, diverse offerings, and the opportunity to snag unique treasures while honing the art of negotiation.

SPECIALTY STORES

Hong Kong's specialty stores cater to niche interests, offering enthusiasts and collectors a haven for discovering unique items and indulging in their passions.

Antiques Stores

Cat Street, officially Upper Lascar Row, is renowned for its antique shops, where visitors can unearth treasures ranging from Chinese ceramics and vintage posters to intricate jewelry and ancient artifacts. These stores preserve history through their collections, attracting collectors and history enthusiasts seeking authentic pieces.

Electronics Stores

Sim City in Mong Kok and Apliu Street in Sham Shui Po are hubs for electronics enthusiasts. Sim City houses a maze of stores offering everything from computer components to cameras and gaming consoles, while Apliu Street's flea market-style shops specialize in second-hand electronics, vintage gadgets, and electronic parts, catering to tech aficionados and bargain hunters alike.

These specialty stores offer more than just merchandise; they provide immersive experiences, connecting visitors with their interests while exploring Hong Kong's diverse retail landscape. Whether seeking

119

historical artifacts or cutting-edge gadgets, these stores beckon enthusiasts with their unique offerings, adding depth and character to the city's vibrant shopping scene.

10

DAY TRIPS AND NEARBY ATTRACTIONS

MACAU

Macau offers a plethora of enticing day trip options and nearby attractions, making it an ideal destination for exploration beyond its city limits.

Coloane Island

This serene island is a haven for nature lovers, featuring scenic hiking trails, beautiful beaches like Cheoc Van Beach, and the iconic A-Ma Cultural Village. Visitors can explore the peaceful villages, sample delectable

Portuguese cuisine, and unwind amidst the island's tranquil ambiance.

Taipa Village

This charming neighborhood is known for its preserved colonial architecture, vibrant streets, and rich cultural heritage. Taipa Village is a hub for gastronomy, offering a diverse array of dining experiences, including Macanese cuisine, quaint cafes, and street food stalls.

Cotai Strip

Home to extravagant resorts and entertainment complexes, the Cotai Strip offers a mix of luxury shopping, world-class shows, and thrilling entertainment. The area boasts iconic landmarks like the Venetian Macao, Parisian Macao, and City of Dreams, inviting visitors to indulge in shopping, dining, and entertainment extravaganzas.

Hac Sa Beach

Located on Coloane Island, Hac Sa Beach is famed for its black sand and tranquil shores, offering a serene escape for relaxation and seaside enjoyment.

Macau Tower

This iconic landmark offers breathtaking panoramic views of the cityscape and beyond. Thrill-seekers can partake in activities like the Skywalk, Skyjump, and bungee jumping, while others can savor dining with a view at the tower's revolving restaurant.

With its diverse array of attractions, from natural beauty to cultural experiences and thrilling entertainment, Macau's nearby destinations and day trips promise a fulfilling and varied experience for travelers seeking exploration beyond the city's bustling core.

SHENZHEN

Shenzhen, neighboring Hong Kong, entices travelers with its dynamic attractions, offering an array of day trip options and nearby attractions.

Splendid China Folk Culture Village

This theme park showcases China's rich cultural heritage, featuring miniature replicas of famous landmarks, ethnic villages, and traditional performances. Visitors can immerse themselves in China's diverse culture in a single destination.

Window of the World

Adjacent to Splendid China, this theme park exhibits replicas of global landmarks, allowing visitors to explore miniature versions of iconic sites like the Eiffel Tower, Taj Mahal, and Egyptian pyramids within a single location.

Dafen Oil Painting Village

Art enthusiasts flock to this village, known for its vast collection of art galleries and studios. Visitors can witness artists creating replicas and original artwork, purchase affordable art pieces, or even commission custom paintings.

Shenzhen Bay Park

A serene escape, this waterfront park offers stunning views of Shenzhen Bay and lush greenery. Visitors can stroll along the promenade, engage in outdoor activities, or simply relax amidst nature's beauty.

Luohu Commercial City

This bustling shopping complex is a haven for bargain hunters. With multiple floors of vendors selling a variety of goods like clothing, electronics, and souvenirs, it's a paradise for shoppers seeking deals.

Shenzhen's diverse attractions cater to various interests, from cultural immersion to shopping and leisurely strolls in scenic parks, making it an appealing day trip destination for travelers from Hong Kong looking to explore a different facet of China's vibrant culture and modernity.

GUANGZHOU

Guangzhou, a bustling metropolis within reach of Hong Kong, offers an array of captivating day trip options and nearby attractions that showcase its rich history, cultural heritage, and modern marvels.

Canton Tower

Dominating the skyline, the Canton Tower is an iconic landmark offering panoramic views of the city from its observation decks. Visitors can admire the cityscape by day or experience the dazzling night view from this architectural marvel.

Chimelong Paradise

This sprawling amusement park caters to thrill-seekers with its exhilarating rides, entertaining shows, and family-friendly attractions. It's an ideal destination for those seeking an adrenaline rush and a day filled with fun and excitement.

Yuexiu Park

A serene oasis amidst the urban hustle, Yuexiu Park boasts scenic landscapes, historic sites like the Zhenhai Tower, and tranquil lakes. Visitors can enjoy leisurely walks, admire the iconic Five Rams Statue, and explore the park's cultural relics.

Shamian Island

Known for its European-style buildings and tree-lined avenues, Shamian Island offers a glimpse into Guangzhou's colonial past. Its charming ambiance, historical architecture, and riverside promenade make it a picturesque spot for leisurely strolls and photography.

Chen Clan Ancestral Hall

This architectural masterpiece showcases traditional Cantonese craftsmanship with its intricate wood carvings, ornate decorations, and cultural exhibits, providing insights into local art and history.

Guangzhou's diverse attractions offer a blend of modern entertainment, historical sites, and natural beauty, making it an enticing day trip destination for visitors from Hong Kong seeking to delve into China's cultural tapestry and vibrant city life.

LANTAU ISLAND

Lantau Island, a serene and picturesque destination near Hong Kong, beckons travelers with its natural beauty, cultural landmarks, and tranquil landscapes.

Tian Tan Buddha (Big Buddha)

The iconic Tian Tan Buddha, perched atop Ngong Ping Plateau, is a spiritual and architectural marvel. Visitors can ascend the

268 steps to reach the statue and admire its majestic presence while enjoying panoramic views of the surrounding mountains and sea.

Ngong Ping 360

This scenic cable car ride offers breathtaking views as it traverses from Tung Chung to Ngong Ping Village. The journey showcases Lantau's lush landscapes, and visitors can explore attractions like the Po Lin Monastery and Wisdom Path upon arrival.

Po Lin Monastery

Nestled near the Big Buddha, this serene monastery showcases intricate architecture, peaceful gardens, and sacred artifacts, providing a glimpse into Buddhist culture and offering a tranquil retreat.

Lantau Trail

Nature enthusiasts can embark on hiking adventures along the Lantau Trail, which winds through lush forests, secluded beaches, and scenic vistas. The trail offers various routes, catering to different hiking levels and providing an opportunity to immerse in Lantau's natural beauty.

Tai O Fishing Village

Known for its stilt houses and traditional way of life, Tai O offers a glimpse into Hong Kong's fishing heritage. Visitors can explore its narrow alleys, savor local seafood, and take boat tours to observe the unique village architecture.

Lantau Island's blend of cultural landmarks, natural beauty, and outdoor activities makes it an ideal day trip destination from Hong Kong, inviting travelers to explore its serene landscapes and cultural treasures.

11

PRACTICAL

INFORMATION

SAFETY TIPS

When traveling to Hong Kong, a few practical safety tips can ensure a smooth and secure journey in this vibrant city.

Stay Informed at all times: Keep abreast of local news and any travel advisories. Stay informed about ongoing events, protests, or demonstrations that might affect certain areas.

Be Vigilant in Crowded Places: Hong Kong can get bustling, especially in tourist areas. Keep an eye on your belongings, particularly in crowded places like markets, public transportation, and busy streets. Use anti-theft bags or pouches to keep valuables secure.

Use Licensed Transportation: Opt for registered taxis, official public transport, or reputable ride-hailing services. Ensure the meter is used or agree on a fare before starting the ride.

Health Precautions: Maintain good hygiene practices, especially during flu seasons or health crises. Carry hand sanitizers, tissues, and masks, especially in crowded places.

Beware of Scams: Be cautious of scams or unauthorized agents offering deals or tours. Stick to reputable establishments for tours, accommodations, and purchases.

Respect Local Laws: Hong Kong has specific regulations, especially regarding public demonstrations and protests. Stay away from these areas if they arise.

Emergency Preparedness: Keep emergency contact numbers handy, including local emergency services and the nearest embassy or consulate. Familiarize yourself with basic phrases in Cantonese or carry a translation app for ease of communication.

Travel Insurance: Consider comprehensive travel insurance covering medical emergencies, trip cancellations, and lost belongings.

COVID-19 Safety Measures: Follow local guidelines concerning COVID-19, including mask-wearing in public spaces, social distancing, and any other regulations in place.

By staying informed, practicing vigilance, and respecting local laws and customs, travelers can navigate Hong Kong safely and enjoy their visit to the fullest.

MONEY AND CURRENCY EXCHANGE

When traveling to Hong Kong, managing money and currency exchanges can be straightforward with a few practical tips. The official currency is the Hong Kong Dollar (HKD), and cash is widely accepted, especially in local markets and smaller establishments.

Currency Exchange: Airports, banks, hotels, and authorized money changers offer currency exchange services. Compare rates and fees before converting money to get the best deal. Avoid exchanging currency at unlicensed or unfamiliar places.

ATMs and Credit Cards: ATMs are prevalent and accept international cards like Visa and Mastercard. Check with your bank about international transaction fees and inform them of your travel plans to avoid card issues. Credit cards are widely accepted in upscale restaurants, hotels and larger stores.

Carrying Cash: While credit cards are convenient, having some cash is advisable for smaller vendors, markets, and transportation. Ensure you have smaller denominations for convenience.

Local Costs: Hong Kong is considered relatively expensive, especially in tourist areas. Budget accordingly for dining, attractions, and shopping.

Safety Measures: Carry money in a secure travel wallet or pouch to prevent theft. Be mindful of your surroundings when withdrawing cash from ATMs.

Currency Conversion Apps: Use currency conversion apps or websites to track exchange rates in real-time, enabling informed spending decisions.

Navigating currency exchanges in Hong Kong is manageable with a mix of cash, cards, and smart financial planning, ensuring a hassle-free and enjoyable trip while managing expenses effectively.

COMMUNICATION AND INTERNET ACCESS

Communicating and staying connected in Hong Kong is convenient due to widespread

English usage and excellent internet access across the city.

English Language: English is commonly spoken in Hong Kong, especially in tourist areas, hotels, restaurants, and shops. Most signage, menus, and transportation announcements are in English as well as Chinese (Cantonese and Mandarin).

SIM Cards and Mobile Networks: Purchase local SIM cards from various providers upon arrival at airports, convenience stores, or mobile shops. They offer affordable data plans for internet access and local calls, ensuring connectivity on the go.

Public Wi-Fi: Hong Kong provides free Wi-Fi hotspots in many public places such as shopping malls, parks, and transportation hubs. Look for the "GovWiFi" network for free government-sponsored Wi-Fi access.

Hotel and Accommodation Wi-Fi: Most hotels, hostels, and guesthouses offer complimentary Wi-Fi for guests. Confirm Wi-Fi availability and access details when booking accommodations.

Internet Cafes and Co-Working Spaces: Find internet cafes or co-working spaces in major districts for reliable internet access if needed.

Messaging Apps: Use messaging apps like WhatsApp, WeChat, or Telegram for communication, as they are widely used and reliable for staying in touch with friends, family, or fellow travelers.

Having access to Wi-Fi hotspots, local SIM cards, and the prevalence of English makes staying connected and communicating hassle-free in Hong Kong, allowing travelers to navigate the city and share experiences conveniently.

HEALTH AND MEDICAL SERVICES

Hong Kong offers high-quality healthcare services, making it reassuring for travelers concerned about medical assistance during their visit.

Public Healthcare: The public healthcare system in Hong Kong is renowned for its efficiency and standards. Government hospitals provide emergency care to anyone in need, regardless of nationality. The Queen

Mary Hospital and Prince of Wales Hospital are notable facilities.

Private Healthcare: Private hospitals and clinics cater to locals and expatriates and offer more personalized services. These facilities provide excellent medical care, with English-speaking staff, shorter waiting times, and comfortable amenities. Some renowned private hospitals include Hong Kong Adventist Hospital and Matilda International Hospital.

Medical Insurance: While emergency care is available to all, having comprehensive travel insurance is advisable. It covers medical emergencies, hospitalization, and repatriation, providing financial security and access to private healthcare if needed.

Pharmacies and Medications: Pharmacies, known as "dispensaries," are plentiful in Hong Kong, offering over-the-counter medications and basic healthcare products. Prescriptions may be required for certain medications, so it's wise to carry any necessary prescriptions or medical documents.

COVID-19 Precautions: Hong Kong adheres to stringent COVID-19 safety measures. Follow local guidelines, wear masks in public spaces, maintain social distancing, and stay updated on travel advisories and health alerts.

Being prepared with insurance coverage, knowing healthcare facilities, and adhering to health guidelines ensure a safe and reassuring experience for travelers seeking medical assistance in Hong Kong.

USEFUL PHRASES IN CANTONESE

Mastering some fundamental Cantonese phrases can significantly enhance your travel experience in Hong Kong, fostering smoother communication and demonstrating appreciation for the local culture. Here's a comprehensive guide to essential phrases:

Greetings

Hello - Neih hou (Nay-ho): A versatile greeting suitable for various contexts, expressing friendliness and respect.

Good morning - jóusàhn (Jow-saan): A polite morning greeting.

Good afternoon - jóutaai (Jow-taai): Use this in the afternoon as a greeting.

Good evening - jóuye (Jow-yeh): An evening greeting.

Basic Conversations

Thank you - Mh'gòi (Muh-goy): Express appreciation and gratitude in everyday interactions.

You're welcome - mhsaaih a (muh-sigh ah): A polite response when someone thanks you.

I'm sorry/excuse me - díjī (Dai-gee): Use this to get someone's attention or apologize.

Yes - hai (High): To affirm or agree.

No - mhai (Muh-high): To indicate a negative response.

I don't understand - néih sīk mm sai (Nay-sik mm sai): Helpful when you're having difficulty comprehending.

Please - qíng (Ching): Use to add politeness when making requests.

At Restaurants and Shopping

How much is this? - Gómmáai a (Gom-mai ah?): Essential for asking about prices.

Where is the restroom? - chìh fong chī hūi (Chi-fong chi hoy): Vital when seeking directions to the restroom.

May I have the bill, please? - m̀h'gòi jé daan (Muh-goy jay daan): Polite request for the bill after dining.

Do you have vegetarian options? - néihgó yí díng sì chí gēi m̀h (Nay-gaw yee ding si chay gay mah?): Useful when inquiring about vegetarian dishes.

Directions and Assistance:

Can you help me? - néih hóng dík m̀hjé (Nay hong dik mah-yeah): When seeking assistance or guidance.

Where is the nearest metro station? - yáuh gáahn gāai chìh fóng máhdaa (Yow gawn gai chi fung ma-dah): To ask for directions to the nearest subway station.

I'm lost - néih hòh chìh mìhn (Nay haw chi min): Use when seeking help to find your way.

Polite Phrases

Thank you for your help - M̀h'gòi néih góng dík (Muh-goy nay gong dik): A polite way to express gratitude for someone's assistance.

I appreciate it - ngóh jí hó (Naw gee haw): To convey appreciation.

Basic Questions:

Do you speak English? - Néih sīk góng jūngwáa m̀sī (Nay-sik gong yung-wah mah?): Useful when seeking English-speaking assistance.

Can I take a photo? - Néih hóng jí siu jī (Nay hong gee seeu gee): Essential when seeking permission to take photographs.

Learning and using these phrases can enhance your interactions, show respect for the local culture, and make your travel experience in Hong Kong more enjoyable and fulfilling. Even attempting a few words in Cantonese can foster positive connections with locals and enrich your journey.

12

CULTURAL ETIQUETTE

AND TIPS

When traveling to Hong Kong, observing certain dos and don'ts can ensure a respectful and enjoyable experience:

DOS

Respect local customs: Hong Kong values traditions—observe and respect local customs, such as covering shoulders when visiting temples.

Use public transportation: The MTR (Mass Transit Railway) is efficient and well-connected. Opt for public transport to navigate the city conveniently.

Try local cuisine: Hong Kong boasts a vibrant food scene. Explore local eateries and savor dim sum, roast meats, and street food delicacies.

Keep cash and cards secure: While Hong Kong is generally safe, practice vigilance with personal belongings, especially in crowded areas.

DON'TS

Avoid littering: Hong Kong maintains cleanliness. Dispose of trash responsibly in designated bins to preserve the city's beauty.

Don't disrespect cultural symbols: Refrain from disrespecting cultural symbols, religious sites, or customs, as it can offend locals.

Don't discuss politics extensively: Political discussions can be sensitive. While Hong Kong values free speech, avoid contentious debates.

Don't disregard local laws: Familiarize yourself with local laws and adhere to them, especially regarding protests and public demonstrations.

Observing these dos and don'ts respects Hong Kong's culture, fosters positive interactions, and ensures a harmonious and respectful visit to this vibrant city.

CULTURAL NORMS AND PRACTICES

When immersing yourself in Hong Kong's culture, understanding and respecting its cultural norms and practices is key to a harmonious experience:

Respect for Elders: Hong Kong values respect for elders. Use polite language and gestures when interacting with older individuals, such as addressing them with proper titles like "Uncle" or "Auntie."

Queuing Etiquette: Hong Kongers value orderliness. Queue patiently in public places, whether for transportation, restaurants, or attractions. Cutting queues is generally frowned upon.

Gift-Giving: When offering gifts, present them with both hands as a sign of respect. Avoid gifting items like clocks, handkerchiefs, or sharp objects, which may symbolize negative connotations.

Dining Customs: Tapping your bowl with chopsticks is considered rude, as it resembles a funeral custom. Place chopsticks across the bowl when finished to signify you're done eating.

Dress Code: While Hong Kong is cosmopolitan, dressing modestly is appreciated when visiting temples or more traditional areas. Casual wear can be worns in most places.

Language: Cantonese is the primary language, but English is widely understood. Attempting a few Cantonese phrases can show respect and may facilitate interactions.

By adhering to these cultural norms, travelers can show respect for Hong Kong's traditions and values, fostering positive interactions and a deeper appreciation for the local culture during their stay.

BONUS

HONG KONG TRAVEL PLANNER

Date:

Location:

Budget:

ITINERARY

TODAY'S LOG

6 AM	
7 AM	
8 AM	
9 AM	
10 AM	
11 AM	
12 PM	
1 PM	
2 PM	
3 PM	
4 PM	
5 PM	
6 PM	
7 PM	
8 PM	
9 PM	
10 PM	
11 PM	

PLACES TO GO

- [ ]
- [ ]
- [ ]
- [ ]

LOCAL FOODS TO TRY

- [ ]
- [ ]
- [ ]
- [ ]

HONG KONG TRAVEL PLANNER

Date:

Location:

Budget:

TODAY'S LOG

6 AM	
7 AM	
8 AM	
9 AM	
10 AM	
11 AM	
12 PM	
1 PM	
2 PM	
3 PM	
4 PM	
5 PM	
6 PM	
7 PM	
8 PM	
9 PM	
10 PM	
11 PM	

PLACES TO GO

- ☐
- ☐
- ☐
- ☐

LOCAL FOODS TO TRY

- ☐
- ☐
- ☐
- ☐

HONG KONG TRAVEL PLANNER

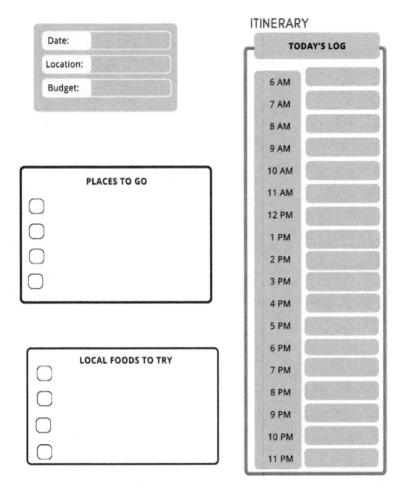

Date:

Location:

Budget:

ITINERARY

TODAY'S LOG

6 AM	
7 AM	
8 AM	
9 AM	
10 AM	
11 AM	
12 PM	
1 PM	
2 PM	
3 PM	
4 PM	
5 PM	
6 PM	
7 PM	
8 PM	
9 PM	
10 PM	
11 PM	

PLACES TO GO

LOCAL FOODS TO TRY

HONG KONG TRAVEL PLANNER

Date:

Location:

Budget:

ITINERARY

TODAY'S LOG

PLACES TO GO

- [ ]
- [ ]
- [ ]
- [ ]

LOCAL FOODS TO TRY

- [ ]
- [ ]
- [ ]
- [ ]

6 AM	
7 AM	
8 AM	
9 AM	
10 AM	
11 AM	
12 PM	
1 PM	
2 PM	
3 PM	
4 PM	
5 PM	
6 PM	
7 PM	
8 PM	
9 PM	
10 PM	
11 PM	

HONG KONG TRAVEL PLANNER

ITINERARY

Date:	
Location:	
Budget:	

TODAY'S LOG

PLACES TO GO

- ☐
- ☐
- ☐
- ☐

6 AM	
7 AM	
8 AM	
9 AM	
10 AM	
11 AM	
12 PM	
1 PM	
2 PM	
3 PM	
4 PM	
5 PM	
6 PM	
7 PM	
8 PM	
9 PM	
10 PM	
11 PM	

LOCAL FOODS TO TRY

- ☐
- ☐
- ☐
- ☐

HONG KONG TRAVEL PLANNER

Date:

Location:

Budget:

ITINERARY

TODAY'S LOG

PLACES TO GO
- [ ]
- [ ]
- [ ]
- [ ]

LOCAL FOODS TO TRY
- [ ]
- [ ]
- [ ]
- [ ]

6 AM	
7 AM	
8 AM	
9 AM	
10 AM	
11 AM	
12 PM	
1 PM	
2 PM	
3 PM	
4 PM	
5 PM	
6 PM	
7 PM	
8 PM	
9 PM	
10 PM	
11 PM	

HONG KONG TRAVEL PLANNER

Date:

Location:

Budget:

ITINERARY

PLACES TO GO

- [ ]
- [ ]
- [ ]
- [ ]

LOCAL FOODS TO TRY

- [ ]
- [ ]
- [ ]
- [ ]

TODAY'S LOG

6 AM	
7 AM	
8 AM	
9 AM	
10 AM	
11 AM	
12 PM	
1 PM	
2 PM	
3 PM	
4 PM	
5 PM	
6 PM	
7 PM	
8 PM	
9 PM	
10 PM	
11 PM	

HONG KONG TRAVEL PLANNER

Date:

Location:

Budget:

ITINERARY

TODAY'S LOG

PLACES TO GO

- [ ]
- [ ]
- [ ]
- [ ]

LOCAL FOODS TO TRY

- [ ]
- [ ]
- [ ]
- [ ]

6 AM	
7 AM	
8 AM	
9 AM	
10 AM	
11 AM	
12 PM	
1 PM	
2 PM	
3 PM	
4 PM	
5 PM	
6 PM	
7 PM	
8 PM	
9 PM	
10 PM	
11 PM	

HONG KONG TRAVEL PLANNER

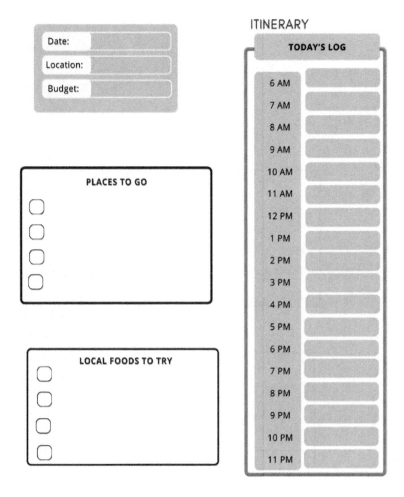

Date:

Location:

Budget:

PLACES TO GO

LOCAL FOODS TO TRY

ITINERARY

TODAY'S LOG

6 AM
7 AM
8 AM
9 AM
10 AM
11 AM
12 PM
1 PM
2 PM
3 PM
4 PM
5 PM
6 PM
7 PM
8 PM
9 PM
10 PM
11 PM

163

HONG KONG TRAVEL PLANNER

Date:

Location:

Budget:

ITINERARY

TODAY'S LOG

PLACES TO GO

- [ ]
- [ ]
- [ ]
- [ ]

LOCAL FOODS TO TRY

- [ ]
- [ ]
- [ ]
- [ ]

6 AM	
7 AM	
8 AM	
9 AM	
10 AM	
11 AM	
12 PM	
1 PM	
2 PM	
3 PM	
4 PM	
5 PM	
6 PM	
7 PM	
8 PM	
9 PM	
10 PM	
11 PM	

HONG KONG TRAVEL PLANNER

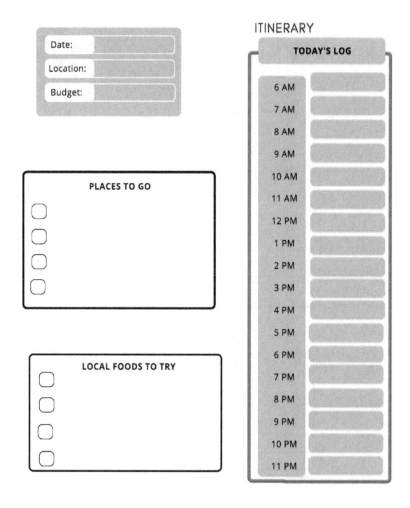

Date:

Location:

Budget:

ITINERARY

TODAY'S LOG

PLACES TO GO

LOCAL FOODS TO TRY

Time
6 AM
7 AM
8 AM
9 AM
10 AM
11 AM
12 PM
1 PM
2 PM
3 PM
4 PM
5 PM
6 PM
7 PM
8 PM
9 PM
10 PM
11 PM

HONG KONG TRAVEL PLANNER

Date:

Location:

Budget:

ITINERARY

TODAY'S LOG

6 AM	
7 AM	
8 AM	
9 AM	
10 AM	
11 AM	
12 PM	
1 PM	
2 PM	
3 PM	
4 PM	
5 PM	
6 PM	
7 PM	
8 PM	
9 PM	
10 PM	
11 PM	

PLACES TO GO

- [ ]
- [ ]
- [ ]
- [ ]

LOCAL FOODS TO TRY

- [ ]
- [ ]
- [ ]
- [ ]

HONG KONG TRAVEL PLANNER

Date:

Location:

Budget:

ITINERARY

TODAY'S LOG

6 AM	
7 AM	
8 AM	
9 AM	
10 AM	
11 AM	
12 PM	
1 PM	
2 PM	
3 PM	
4 PM	
5 PM	
6 PM	
7 PM	
8 PM	
9 PM	
10 PM	
11 PM	

PLACES TO GO

- ☐
- ☐
- ☐
- ☐

LOCAL FOODS TO TRY

- ☐
- ☐
- ☐
- ☐

HONG KONG TRAVEL PLANNER

Date:

Location:

Budget:

ITINERARY

TODAY'S LOG

6 AM	
7 AM	
8 AM	
9 AM	
10 AM	
11 AM	
12 PM	
1 PM	
2 PM	
3 PM	
4 PM	
5 PM	
6 PM	
7 PM	
8 PM	
9 PM	
10 PM	
11 PM	

PLACES TO GO

- [ ]
- [ ]
- [ ]
- [ ]

LOCAL FOODS TO TRY

- [ ]
- [ ]
- [ ]
- [ ]

HONG KONG TRAVEL PLANNER

Date:

Location:

Budget:

ITINERARY

TODAY'S LOG

6 AM	
7 AM	
8 AM	
9 AM	
10 AM	
11 AM	
12 PM	
1 PM	
2 PM	
3 PM	
4 PM	
5 PM	
6 PM	
7 PM	
8 PM	
9 PM	
10 PM	
11 PM	

PLACES TO GO

- ☐
- ☐
- ☐
- ☐

LOCAL FOODS TO TRY

- ☐
- ☐
- ☐
- ☐

HONG KONG TRAVEL PLANNER

Date:

Location:

Budget:

ITINERARY

TODAY'S LOG

6 AM	
7 AM	
8 AM	
9 AM	
10 AM	
11 AM	
12 PM	
1 PM	
2 PM	
3 PM	
4 PM	
5 PM	
6 PM	
7 PM	
8 PM	
9 PM	
10 PM	
11 PM	

PLACES TO GO

☐
☐
☐
☐

LOCAL FOODS TO TRY

☐
☐
☐
☐

HONG KONG TRAVEL PLANNER

Date:

Location:

Budget:

ITINERARY

PLACES TO GO

LOCAL FOODS TO TRY

TODAY'S LOG

6 AM

7 AM

8 AM

9 AM

10 AM

11 AM

12 PM

1 PM

2 PM

3 PM

4 PM

5 PM

6 PM

7 PM

8 PM

9 PM

10 PM

11 PM

HONG KONG TRAVEL PLANNER

Date:

Location:

Budget:

ITINERARY

PLACES TO GO

☐
☐
☐
☐

LOCAL FOODS TO TRY

☐
☐
☐
☐

TODAY'S LOG

6 AM	
7 AM	
8 AM	
9 AM	
10 AM	
11 AM	
12 PM	
1 PM	
2 PM	
3 PM	
4 PM	
5 PM	
6 PM	
7 PM	
8 PM	
9 PM	
10 PM	
11 PM	

HONG KONG TRAVEL PLANNER

Date:

Location:

Budget:

ITINERARY

TODAY'S LOG

6 AM

7 AM

8 AM

9 AM

10 AM

11 AM

12 PM

1 PM

2 PM

3 PM

4 PM

5 PM

6 PM

7 PM

8 PM

9 PM

10 PM

11 PM

PLACES TO GO

LOCAL FOODS TO TRY

173

HONG KONG TRAVEL PLANNER

Date:

Location:

Budget:

ITINERARY

TODAY'S LOG

PLACES TO GO

- [ ]
- [ ]
- [ ]
- [ ]

LOCAL FOODS TO TRY

- [ ]
- [ ]
- [ ]
- [ ]

6 AM	
7 AM	
8 AM	
9 AM	
10 AM	
11 AM	
12 PM	
1 PM	
2 PM	
3 PM	
4 PM	
5 PM	
6 PM	
7 PM	
8 PM	
9 PM	
10 PM	
11 PM	

Printed in Great Britain
by Amazon